I'm FEELING (a little bit) SHY

Managing Designer: Nicola Butler
With expert advice from Dr. Angharad Rudkin, Clinical Psychologist

I'm FEELING (a Little bit) SHY

Anna Milbourne

Illustrated by Åsa Gilland

Designed by Anna Gould

You may have been expecting
to meet someone on this page...

But this is a book about feeling shy.
And the thing about feeling shy is,
it's really tricky to meet people and to say...

···hello.

Not ALL hellos are tricky. Saying hello to my friend I've known FOREVER is easy.

"Hi, Lara. Let's play!"

And saying hello to my uncle normally goes something like this...
"OOF!"

But sometimes, when grown-ups all stare down at me and say **HELLO**, I can't answer (even if that's rude). My mouth feels stuck and I feel very SMALL..

sometimes,
to walk into a
of children too.

Especially if they all look at once.
It makes me wish I could just...

...disap

My big brother can say hello to anyone - and

When he sees new people, he jumps right in and invents a fun game and plays and plays. And soon everyone is laughing and having fun.

"Hello, everyone here! Let's play round-and-round-about **spaceship adventures!**"

Mostly, I stay quietly by myself so no one notices me. But sometimes...

I slip into the game when no one's looking, and start playing too.

"All aboard the spaceship! Next stop, Planet Whirligig!"

And then, once I'm past that shy feeling, I'm all happy and I'm not quiet or hide-y any more.

I'm chitter-chattery...

non-stop dancy...

...happy,
bouncy
me!

"Hi, Charlie!"

And I don't even think
about it till the next time.

At my friend Lara's birthday party, Mummy says, "Go on in."
But the party room is so full, I'm scared to go by myself.

"Awww, are you SHY?"
Lara's granny says.

And I turn red. It's like I'm in a box
called SHY and stuck there forever.
But then Mummy says, "When she's
ready, she'd love to join in."

And Lara is so happy to see me, she squeals.
I give her the present and she puts it with the others.

"Thanks! Come on," she says, and runs
off. But I can't let go of Mummy's hand.

"I might not," I whisper when Mummy bends down.
I feel glued to the spot. I don't feel like joining in at all.

"You're not ready yet –
that's okay," says Mummy.
"Let's have a look first.
Can you see Lara?"

I nod.

"Why don't we pop in
together and give her
the present?" she says.

And I really want to give Lara the present because I chose
it and it's a unicorn and she's going to love it. So I take a
deep breath and we step through the door.

And by the end of the party, I've forgotten I was feeling shy at all. I'm playing games and singing Happy Birthday and I'm happy in the middle of all that fun.

After the party, Mummy takes me to buy new shoes.
I'm starting a new school on Monday.

I won't know anyone in my class. I'm really scared.
"I don't want to GO," I tell Mummy.
And then my feelings all burst out...

"What if
NO ONE wants
to be my FRIEND?"

Mummy gives me a cuddle.
"You're feeling nervous. That's
natural – going to a new school
is exciting and full of unknown
things. But you're going to
be okay. You'll see."

My brother is already at that school. "You know what?" he tells me later. "I was scared too before I went. And now I have a class full of awesome friends. I couldn't even imagine them before."

"But YOU'RE never scared of talking to ANYONE!"

"I am," he laughs, "all the time! But I don't like that feeling, so I try to skip over it to the fun part!"

Mummy tells me, "EVERYONE feels a little bit shy sometimes. But as you grow up, you can learn ways to get past it to the good part - having fun!"

"How do I get past it?" I ask.

"Some people like to be quiet at first and just watch and listen. And that's okay. You can take your time. Then, when you're ready, you can join in."

As I snuggle down to sleep, I tell Sookie Sloth, "EVERYONE feels a little bit shy sometimes."

And somehow that makes me feel a little tiny bit better.

In the morning, we are walking to the new school.

My tummy feels all flittery-fluttery.

"It's called having butterflies,"
Mummy tells me.

"EEK!"

Mummy laughs.
"They aren't REAL butterflies.
It's your body's way of getting
ready to meet new people.
The butterflies are tickling you
to keep you on the look-out!"

"On the look-out for what?" I say.

"For new friends! Maybe you'll see someone drawing a sloth because they LOVE sloths..."

"I love sloths too! Maybe we could play together."

"Exactly. You don't know who you'll find yet, but you're sure to find some really nice people."

And all of a sudden, we're at school. Mummy drops me off in the class. And my butterflies flutter and help me pay attention to EVERYTHING.

When everyone clusters around me, I feel too shy to speak...

Then I notice one quiet girl with a unicorn bag.

She gives me a little **wave,**

so I **wave** back.

After lunch, I sit next to the girl who waved, and I ask her if she likes unicorns (even though my voice comes out all small and whispery).

She says, "Yes, a lot!" So I draw her my best unicorn. And she draws friendly hearts and stars.

Before I know it, Mummy
is waiting to pick me up.
"How did it go?"

"I thought nobody would want
to be my friend, but now
I think I might have a WHOLE
CLASS of new friends!"

I give a big happy sigh of relief.
"I can't wait to come back tomorrow!"

So you know what?
Sometimes, I feel a little bit shy.
But that's okay. Everyone does.

If you ever feel a little bit shy too, be brave.
Plunge in or take your time, but go ahead and try.
You can find your own way through the shy feeling
to the fun part, with lots of new friends!